SERIOUS ANGEL

SERIOUS ANGEL

A SELECTION OF POEMS BY

JAN TWARDOWSKI

TRANSLATED FROM THE POLISH BY

SARAH LAWSON
&
MAŁGORZATA KORASZEWSKA

WAXWING SERIES NO. 3

DEDALUS

The Dedalus Press
24 The Heath ~ Cypress Downs ~ Dublin 6W
Ireland

ISBN   1 904556 17 5
Edition limited to 350 copies

Dedalus Press books are represented and distributed in the
U.S.A. and Canada by **Dufour Editions Ltd** P.O. Box 7,
Chester Springs, Pennsylvania 19425
in the UK by **Central Books** 99 Wallis Road, London E9 5LN

The Dedalus Press receives financial assistance from
An Chomhairle Ealaíon, The Arts Council, Ireland.

Printed in Dublin by Johnswood Press

Introduction

Jan Twardowski (1915-) is the best-loved poet in Poland. Even people who do not usually read poetry light up at the mention of his name and quote you a few lines. He has been writing and publishing prolifically since 1959, and his books have sold in the hundreds of thousands, yet he has been almost completely unknown in the English-speaking world.

Jan Twardowski is a retired priest who still lives in Warsaw, where he officiated at the Church of the Visitation in Krakowskie Przedmiescie Street for many years. He had always combined poetry with his priestly vocation, but he came to national prominence in 1970 with the publication of *Znaki ufnosci* (The Signs of Trust) which contained his poem "Explanation", beginning "I didn't come to convert you". This poem had an immediate effect on readers. Here was a priest who freely admitted that he did not have all the answers and that he was sometimes just as mystified and as troubled as his parishioners. "I will not pour holy theology into your ear with a teaspoon," he promises. Rather, he will confide his secret: "that I, a priest / believe God like a child."

When he writes about death, love, and loss, he writes frankly as a man who has experienced them himself and understands the pain of others. His poems are simple — at least on the surface — and full of concrete images and startling juxtapositions. Father Twardowski has said somewhere that he collects books about animals and likes to read about them, and it shows in his poetry. A collection of his poems is a veritable zoo of every imaginable kind of animal.

5

There is a pleasing sense of humour in evidence in many of his poems; an amusing turn of phrase, a witty play on words, or a surprising, aphoristic, final line may turn a solemn poem into a more playful one.. For all the serious concerns of most of his poems, in "About the Little Ones" Jan Twardowski observes small restless children during a sermon with great affection and understanding. Nothing and no one is too small to attract his interest.

Father Twardowski's wry humour and simplicity may almost make you forget that he is often writing about the most profound mysteries of the Christian faith. He tackles the great subjects of human life and gets to the emotional essence of them. One of his deceptively simple devices is that of paradox. The Creator, he says in "A Childless Angel", "created the world so good / that it's imperfect / and you so imperfect / that you're good". God is omnipotent but sometimes absent ("The Absent One Is"); or God is omnipotent but humble ("Humble"), or even purposely invisible: "God went into hiding so that the world could be seen" ("The World").

It has been a pleasure for me to work on these poems with my co-translator, Malgorzata Koraszewska, and a pleasure for us both to enable Jan Twardowski to reach a wider, non-Polish, public.

Sarah Lawson: London
2003

Contents

Sunt Lacrimae Rerum ut Mentem Mortalia Tangunt

They remained alone
a thimble
a soup bowl and a dinner plate
the merry grandma's little mirror
three silver forks
a cock made of red clay
photos with a heart condition
a not bad funeral joke
a name on the grave

Things are wailing after you.

No

Do not sprinkle sugar on religion
do not smudge her with an eraser

do not put pink rags on angels flying above a war
do not refer the faithful to the shepherd's pipe
                              of commentary
I am not coming for comfort as for a bowl of soup
I wanted finally to support my head
on the stone of faith

At the Tail End

Finally at the tail-end
save theologians
so they will not eat up all the candles and sit in darkness
will not rap a rose on the knuckles
will not cut the Gospel into slices
will not tug holy words by their nerves
will not cut reeds for fishing rods
will not quarrel among themselves
will not parade on a hippopotamus of Latin
so they will not be surprised
that a helpless warbling lisp of faith
leads to heaven

Request

Holy Virgin drawn in an exercise book
by a child's hands —
beautiful like one stroke
pray for us

so that there will be no embroidered napkins in churches
a catafalque with a black cover
an angel with a little baroque paw
banners with brushy fringes
clattering money
trinkets with skulls and crossbones
Saint Theresa like a spoiled starlet

saints not like themselves
who cannot get away from not-their-faces —
so that there will not be
a nice, neatly combed Lord Jesus for decent people only

He Looked

He looked
at Gothic which keeps making medieval faces
at the 18th-century altar like a baroque coffin
                                        on little rat paws
at a shaggy carpet which converts our steps into stealthy cats
at a chandelier like a great lady in a crinoline
at an illustrious ceiling
at proudly penitential kneelers
at an angel always one size too small
at leaves which look black in the light of the red lamp

He stood in the corner
he took his hands from the cross and wrung them
and thought
surely all this is not for me

Overheard and Noted Down

The door trembled : "Who's there?"
"Death."
He came in, tiny
Little with a scythe like a matchstick.
Astonishment. Eyes out on stalks.
And he :
"I came for the canary."

The World

God went into hiding so that the world could be seen
if he were to reveal himself he would be alone
who would dare to notice an ant
a beautiful wicked wasp bustling around
a green drake with yellow legs
a lapwing which lays only four eggs
a dragonfly's rounded eyes and beans in pods
our mother at the table who so recently
lifted a cup by its long funny handle
a fir which does not cast cones but husks
suffering and delight both sources of knowledge
secrets not smaller but always different
rocks that show travellers the way

an invisible love
does not block the view

Why

Why
did you create
our joy, anxiety,
our despair and wit,
our happiness, unhappiness
out of nothing

Trees are Non Believers

Every single tree is a non-believer
birds do not learn religion at all
a dog very seldom goes to church
they really know nothing
yet so obedient

insects under bark do not know the Gospel
even white caraway most silent along the path
common field stones
like crooked tears on a face
do not know Franciscans
yet so poor

righteous stars do not want to listen to my sermons
lilies-of-the-valley on the edge therefore lonely
all mountains quiet and as patient as faith
various loves with cardiac defects
yet so pure

I Do Not Fabricate

I write what I see I do not fabricate anything
a crane's legs grow even faster than its wings
a raven builds two nests for variety
a black alder casts off green leaves
a daisy sometimes has ninety-eight petals
like Plato every ordinary piglet loves us
the Invisible carries me like a listless chicken
dogs don't howl — that means they're surprised too
it is late time for a prayer
forget me amen.

Humble

God omnipotent but so humble
He is everywhere but seen nowhere
He is hanging on to the cross with both hands
pure because of having everything He has nothing
                                        for Himself
He hears patiently that He will be of no further use

only the Almighty can be so small
still they say to Him out of spite
that He has a Jew for a Son

Explanation

I did not come to convert you
anyway all the wise sermons escaped from my head
for a long time I have been stripped of my glitter
like a hero in slow motion
I will not badger you
asking what you think about Merton
I will not hop about during the discussion like a turkey
with a red drop on its nose
I will not grow beautiful like a drake in October
I will not dictate tears admitting everything
I will not pour holy theology into your ear with a teaspoon

I will just sit beside you
and confide in you my secret
that I, a priest
believe God like a child.

When Great Art is too Great

Lord Jesus I think You don't like being tortured with organs
                                      in churches
You've had enough of Bach's music —
maybe you would like to hear
how a Hebrew letter creaks in the Bible on its black legs
how confessors murmur straight into the ear of conscience
a growing halo above a saint hurts
furtive eyes cry
shoes after rain drip on the floor
grandma yawns over a litany
a snowy goldfinch hops on tram stops
over a candle in a candlestick
one burning match squeaks

Even with a violin we do not hear the strings but the case

Words

To the last moment he never stopped talking
as if he wanted to drag his tongue beyond death
kneeling by his bed I explained to him
that words mean nothing there
they don't bother anybody
you can't demand any fee for them
they're as out-of-date as an old campaigner who still marches
                                                 as he walks
they lie no longer than they live
they're as awkward as an unlicked calf

I explained that awaiting him
is just one word which is silence

The Absent One Is

God is so great that He is and He is not
so omnipotent that He is capable of not being
therefore His absence also happens
hence there is sometimes darkness and hearts rattle
and will even whimper like an impatient dog

even believers do not believe quietly
and want with a joke to slip away from emotion
though so shortly before they believed by rote
that you wait your whole life for the moment

but God is so great that sometimes He is not
the brain bows like a tulip with fatigue
and thoughts run on a common empty path
like ladybirds gathering
to hide before the despair of winter
only silence remains and stars above
and the moon righteous because it's completely naked
and dragonflies so minute that they know it all
and the last leaf buzzes directly from the poplar
that the Absent One is
because it hurts more

A Childless Angel

Just when you were thinking
that parrots live longer
that you are terribly small
useless like a fake fire-place
in the dining room
like a childless angel
light like two pence change
second best genius
when you surrounded yourself with books
like a sick man
not believing that from nonbelief
arises a new belief
that those who went away once again
will abandon you
holy and full of mistakes

just then you were chosen by Somebody Who is greater
                                        than you yourself
Who created the world so good
that it's imperfect
and you so imperfect
that you're good

About a Sparrow

I don't know how to write about a church
about tents of prayers over masses and altars
about a clock gnawing at us
about a saint with a haircut like grass
about windows that throw in butterflies
like colourful little ships
about moths like black breath soiling the candles
about the eye of Providence
which sees nuts that are hard to crack
about Our Lady's hair made entirely of warm wind
about those who are sorry even before they sin

but about somebody
hidden in the shadow
who suddenly is light hot like July from tears
goes away transformed into a sensitive heart of violins
and about you wayward sparrow
that astonished by Grace
tumbled
into the holy water

About the Little Ones

Only the little ones were not bored during the sermon
all the time they had something to do
they tamed dead umbrellas protruding from the pews
                                    with envious paws
they knelt over the glasses case dropped by a grandmother
                          as though it were a ground beetle
they stuck out their pink tongues
they scratched the sinners on the moustaches of their
shoelaces
they were surprised that a priest wears trousers
that somebody took off a lace mitten and dressed her fat hand
                                        in holy water
they counted the pious legs of the ladies
they organised a competition for picking up a pin by its head
they sniffed at something squeaking in the missal
money for the collection they hid for ice cream
they stamped on the clock from which wasps of minutes
                                        disperse
they climbed like a finch on pines to see
what was going on up between the sleeve
and the collar
like a phonetician they pronounced an open astonished "O"
when the priest stuttered in the pulpit

— but Jesus took them solemnly on His lap

I Am Afraid of Your Love

I am not afraid of a brass band at the end of the world
biblical stamping
I am afraid of Your love
for You love quite differently
so close and different
like an ant in front of a bear
You place crosses like soldiers who are too tall
You do not look with my eyes
maybe You see like a bee
for whom white lilies are blue-green
You avoid the questioner as though he were a hedgehog
                                     on Your stroll
You announce that purity is giving away oneself
You bring people close together
and constantly teach how to go away
You talk too often to those who are alive
the dead are going to explain

I am afraid of Your love
the one most true and different

Nothing More

He wrote "My God" but crossed out because he thought
                                        after all
it's only *my* if I am selfish
he wrote "God of humanity" but bit his tongue because
                                        he remembered
the angels and stones looking like rabbits in the snow
finally he wrote "God". Nothing more
Still he wrote too much

Before a Journey

You, who do not protect from disappointments
who do not guard against the pitfalls of human love
who give as if You were begging
who do not cure cancer
who feed with hunger
who do not give a life insurance policy
who do not put wounds on a silk cushion
who stationed angels with swords at the gates of Paradise
and not diplomats in white gloves
I still believe
that You lift up our wrung gnarled fingers
open our eyes red like rabbits'
turn the light on
explain
on the other side
everybody has his long journey

A Serious Angel but not Serious Questions

Have you become an angel only after long thought
do your fingers caress or only point
do you confess only heavy sins because the light ones are
                                                hard to bear
do you clap your hands looking at death throes as if a goal
                                        were about to be scored
do you never cry so as never to smile
can you listen attentively without a reason
do you not snuggle in order to go away
don't you pine for a body
for a human smile
for hands to put together
for a chaffinch that leaves gardens in September
for a foal closing its eyes
for a beetle with yellow and red legs
for every second always being the last
for what is impermanent and therefore precious

About Pain

What pain can change into
into anger into stamping your foot
into an open book closed slowly
into a prayer
private crying directly to the pillow
a letter written five times incoherent and nonsensical
silence at the table
pacing up and down around the truth
touching your lonely mouth with a teaspoon
into something impossible — still not the last
into the same love again
taking a long time to end

so allow us Mother
let the pain continue

Ant Dragon Fly Ladybird

Ant which hasn't grown for centuries
moth going from lamp to lamp
by a short cut and the simplest way
fire-fly blinking not known but not strange
grasshopper
drag-free dragon-fly
gaily indifferent
ladybird which even a pope
would ponder with his chin in his hand

I tramp through the world like a heavy elephant
so big that I understand nothing
I think how to kneel
and not have my nose in the air

and our life is equally
uncertain and tiny

The Certainty of Uncertainty

Thank you
for not saying the unsaid
for not finishing the unfinished
for not proving the unproved

thank you
for being sure that you were unsure
for believing in a possible impossibility
for not knowing what to do next in religion lessons
and a tear stuck in your throat like a fruit stone
because being as you are
not talking
you told me so much about God

Saint Nitwit

He loved – but nobody wanted him
he hurried – nobody waited for him
he rattled the door – the wrong person opened it
he ran with his heart – the road came to an end
he still pined for somebody through the garden gate

"she loves you not, she loves you not"
they told him fortunes from petals

and it was empty all around
as if the world said
bless you
just to be polite

I Trusted the Road

I trusted the road
narrow
a head-over-heels kind
with knee-deep holes
the kind that's past its time like late sugarbeets in November
and I went out into a meadow and there stood St. Agnes
"at last," she said
"I was worrying
that you had gone by a different route
a straighter one
on the asphalt
the motorway to heaven – with a travelling fellowship –
and that devils took you"

Happiness

There is no love without a response
the heart stays behind in spite of having gone away
as long as it's not for yourself

then the cow comforts with its tail
the seven-foot gorilla hugs a gorilla
a goat will go to a goat
the kingfisher waits for a king to go fishing
the hedgehog doesn't hedgehop over the hedge-sow
the computer asks the cock what time it is
a stork will tell fortunes with at least one non-Party leg
they are kissing everybody even nobodies
happiness is like a violin the older the younger

* * *

A hare turns white
in order not to perish in the snow
a dung beetle turns green amidst the grasses
in order that death will not catch it
in the summer the sky is blue
just for the sake of beauty
what charm in the impractical

Sarah Lawson was born in Indianapolis in 1943 and holds degrees in English from Indiana University, the University of Pennsylvania, and Glasgow University. Her poetry and book reviews have appeared in numerous magazines. Her most recent poetry publication is a pamphlet, *Twelve Scenes of Malta*. She has translated both the medieval feminist Christine de Pisan and the modern surrealist Jacques Prévert from French and is now working on a translation of Cervantes from Spanish. She lives in London.

Małgorzata Koraszewska was born in Uzbekistan in 1943 after her parents were deported from Poland by the Soviets. She grew up in Warsaw and gained a degree in sociology from the University of Warsaw. She worked as a researcher at the Academy of Science in Warsaw and later studied at the University of Lund. While living in London in the 1990s she began translating a variety of English and American fiction and non-fiction into Polish. She now lives in Poland.

Waxwing Series of Limited Edition Booklets
from The Dedalus Press:

No. 1: **"Furnace of Love"** : A Selection from the Religious Poetry of *Tadhg Gaelach Ó Súilleabháin*, translated from the Irish by *Pádraig J. Daly*

No. 2: **"The Life of the Virgin Mary"** : by *Rainer Maria Rilke*, translated from German by *Christine McNeill*